Habakkuk's Hope

Finding your hope story again

Lona Renée Fraser

Heartprint Publishing

Habakkuk's Hope: Finding Your Hope Story Again
By Lona Renee Fraser
Managing Editor: Loral Robben Pepoon, Cowriterpro
Associate Editor: Debi Selby
Prepared for Publication by: Kayla Fioravanti, Selah Press, LLC
Cover Design: Jennifer Smith, Eco-Office Gals
Illustrations: Cherish Driskell
Photography: Karissa Noelle Selby
Printed in the United States of America, Published by Heartprint Publishing
Copyright © 2016 Lona Renee Fraser
ISBN-13: 978-0692641422 (Heartprint Publishing)
ISBN-10: 0692641424

Dedication

This book is dedicated to my mother, Kathy Schumaker, who showed me how to love extravagantly; my father, David G. Schumaker, who instilled in me strong character; my brother, David C. Schumaker, who taught me to never give up; and my husband, Jim Fraser, for being my "silent strength."

I LOVE YOU!

From the Author

Dear Friend,

Every aspect of life, to me, is a story. I have hundreds—from curling my hair to the crazy girl I met at the salon to the dragonfly that visited me every day at the ocean. Life is full of everyday moments. Some moments are easy and care-free, while others are not.

Habakkuk's Hope came out of my desperate cry to the Lord during a time when I was not myself. Too many major events had happened in a short amount of time and those circumstances led me down a path of sadness that turned a corner at loneliness and parked itself at hopelessness.

Healing is a process—it took a while for my heart to sink into hopelessness, and it takes some time to get on the other side of it. But God is a redeemer. And the longings in our heart that we have hurt over for years can be healed, just like our hearts can be restored and rebuilt. But, you can't rush the journey. I know, I felt the same sigh that you may have just as I typed that sentence.

I have a tendency to want to jump ahead and get to the peak of the mountain and sing "the hills are alive" and twirl like Julie Andrews in *The Sound of Music.* Who doesn't? But it is the "ouch" moments, the LOL moments and the ugly-cry moments that take up minutes of the day that lead to years and turn into a lifetime. These moments are all near and dear to our Heavenly Father's heart. They are our journeys.

My prayer is that *Habakkuk's Hope* gets you from here to there—from where you are in your story now, to your next chapter. I'm asking that through it, the Father moves you from hopelessness to wholeness. Thank you for allowing me to share my heart with yours. I have faith that you will find your hope story, and I hope it never ends.

Love,

Contents

Study Guidelines

HAVE FUN: Girl time is always fun time! Cause "Girls Just Wanna Have Fun!"

BE HONEST: If you only process half of your story, you may miss out on receiving complete healing.

BE CONFIDENTIAL: If someone confides in you, keep the information between you, that person and God.

ENCOURAGE: Always try to encourage, lift up and pray for one another.

COMMIT: Schedules are full, but consistency and coming to class is vital. The material is best digested week by week, verse by verse, prayer by prayer journal and by journal.

BE PATIENT: Healing is a process. Give your heart the time it needs to heal.

1

Setting the Stage

My girlfriend can predict when a storm is coming just by how her hip feels. Well, my hip didn't tell me, but my heart did. I didn't know when my storm was coming, but I knew it was approaching and it was different from any other. I remember telling my best friend, *"You are not going to want to be my friend this year."* Then the storm came.

It was the summer before my son's senior year of high school. I wasn't sure how the beginning of empty nesting was going to hit me. You never know how you truly are going to react to big changes in your life until you actually experience them.

I started thinking . . . OK. My. Son. Is. Graduating. And. Going. To. College. I remember it like it was yesterday—the first day of school when Brendan climbed the three large steps that he could barely reach on the small school bus that would take him safely to kindergarten. I sound like my mother when she is reminiscing about my childhood. *Am I really old enough for this to be happening?*

I won't hear him playing drums or asking me to wash the shirt that he wants to wear the next day for school. My compassionate son who asks, *"Mom, do you need a hug?"* Yes, that one. All the little moments that string along without you even taking notice, becoming memories as days turn into months and then years. It's like when an approaching tidal wave crashes over you—you feel a part of yourself dying, with an epic chapter ending and the turning of a page.

The very same year, I turned the big "40." There hadn't been any year that affected me negatively, so I wasn't anticipating the emotional turmoil that lay ahead. I thought, *"There are so many things I didn't accomplish and half my life is over! 40! Are you kidding me? And my son is leaving me!"* Yep. Darkness was coming from all directions aiming straight for my heart.

As time went on, my son and daughter graduated and went on to college. Yes, my sweet Diddly Doo graduated the year after my Pumpkin Pooh did. The silence in the house was deafening. I remember sitting at my kitchen table and all I could hear was the clock ticking so loudly, like a nagging bully, shouting in my face, *"They're gone, remember! They're gone!"*

I had been a mom for 18 years and counting. And though, of course, still a mom, I was no longer needed 24 hours a day, seven days a week. I was more "on call." I didn't know what to do or how to do it anymore. I felt in a daze, stunned, shocked . . . in a twilight zone of sorts. *"How can I be expected to let go so abruptly? How do I move to the sidelines, when I'm used to being in the game?"* It was like having training wheels on again or being a toddler who wobbles and falls repeatedly.

All I have known, and all that was expected, had come to a screeching halt. It's like the end of a rollercoaster ride that you want to end, yet, really you don't. I was expected to train up my child in the way they should go. Go. That's the part breaking my heart, leaving a black hole where "mom" was. I realized, at this point, I wasn't going to get over this quickly. It was going to be a process.

I continued to try and do what I had to do to function. I still had a household to take care of and my husband's business to run. Whatever regrets I had about what I wanted to do, should've done or could've done differently, could not be changed now. I had my time to play and the game was over. I had to accept it and move on. But how—and how do I fill this void in my heart?

I'd like to pause here and just say, I am typically a happy, prayer warring, God hope-filled extrovert, clown of the party, girl with the glass full—no, glass overflowing—encourager, a cheerleader, and I provide the shoulder to cry on. And I have had my share of really hard times, so it's not like this was my first rodeo.

But all that happened was too much, too soon. Let me recap some fun facts. During a three-year period, I turned 40 and my son and daughter graduated from high school and went on to college— it seems like such a simple sentence when I read it, but the devastation it brought to my life was catastrophic. I lost my bearing—and in it, my identity. My mind and heart didn't have the chance to process, rest or transition. I couldn't get off the rollercoaster of emotion no matter how hard I tried.

And I felt alone. I had never felt this way before. I mean, I have felt alone before, but this time was different. Being alone and feeling alone are two completely different things. In a world where family and friends were abundant, it was as if I was Batman with no Robin, Tom Hanks with no Wilson, or Lucille Ball with no Ricky or Ethel—I felt like I had no one to comfort my broken heart or to soothe the ache in my soul. Sadness coupled with loneliness deepened to hopelessness. I was a lost little girl, who needed to find my way back home. And then Habakkuk.

After the 1000th cry, I began to pray. I mean, it's not that I hadn't been praying, but at the level of desperation I was in, the clarity of prayer became a megaphone to my heart, mind and soul. I used different words than before. I was being transformed from the inside out.

It was the appointed time. I was ready to hear what God had to say. It was the safest place for me to be: held in the arms of my Creator, who was gently rocking me from emotional unrest into emotional peace. He cradled my heart. He cradled my mind. He cradled my soul. I needed all three. I threw my anchor out of the ship in the middle of the torrential storm. I had to. He was the only One who could calm the waves threatening to drown me. I had to believe that He had the power to rescue me from this nightmare—and He did. He met my heart in Habakkuk.

My hope for you through this study is that you find yourself in either story—Habakkuk's or mine. I pray that you find hope where you locked the door, threw away the key and put so much furniture up against it that you can't see the door any more. As we walk alongside Habakkuk, I will share how God used his story to touch mine.

My desire is for you to find rest, peace and joy in these pages, between these words. I want you to have hope for your heart again—hope where you thought all hope was lost. My prayer is that you feel God's Presence, page by page, singing His sweet lullaby of love and whispering His eternal hope over you as you find your hope story again.

Notes

God, Why?

What do you think of when you hear the word hope? I think of something to look forward to, along with butterflies and happiness—at least those are my first few thoughts, anyway.

In Merriam-Webster's Dictionary, hope is:
—a desire accompanied by expectation of or belief in fulfillment
—to cherish a desire with anticipation
—to expect with confidence: trust

What are you hoping for? When I teach women's classes, I ask questions to help women identify hopes and longings as well as hurts. During a fun moment in class, I shouted out to the women, *"If you don't have love, what do you have?"* A woman shouted back, *"I have the HOPE of love."* I then asked, *"If you don't have money, what do you have?"* The shout of reply came, *"I have the HOPE of money!"*

You get the gist. God invites you to ask for whatever thing you are hoping for, and He gives you the assurance of receiving that very thing. Pray for it. Claim it in your heart. Proclaim it to others, and see what the Lord will do. I often say:

"There is always hope, because there is always God."

Can I get an AMEN?

"Hope deferred makes the heart sick,
But when the desire comes, it is a tree of life."
Proverbs 13:12

Let's begin the journey of finding hope starting with a little Habakkuk history.

Habakkuk was a minor prophet in the Old Testament. He was courageous and bold, and had a very tender heart of compassion for his people. Not much is known about him personally. What is known is that Habakkuk was not a common Hebrew name like John is today. It's interesting that it means "embrace" or "wrestle." More on that later.

Like his name, Habakkuk was unique. He was a one-of-a-kind prophet. Unlike most prophets, Habakkuk initiated dialogue with God versus God initiating the dialogue. He started a conversation. And it was a deep one at that. The Book of Habakkuk starts out:

"The burden which the prophet Habakkuk saw."
Habakkuk 1:1

What a happy way to begin a story, right?!

Please read Habakkuk 1:1–4.

Habakkuk was extremely concerned for his nation—for his people, the tribe of Judah. He witnessed Judah's demise from the successful rule of King Josiah (640–609 B.C.) to the destructive rule under Josiah's son, King Jehoiakim (609–597 B.C.) Evil was taking over the nation. Major corruption prevailed in the courts; physical violence, constant conflict and mistreatment of the righteous were rampant, as were all forms of idolatry and lawlessness. The rich were exploiting the poor, the strong were abusing the weak—and on and on it went.

In verse two, Habakkuk cries out for God to help his people with no reply—so Habakkuk asks again more passionately. The first cry is translated "to cry for help," and the second means to cry out loud with a disturbed heart. I don't know about you, but I TOTALLY get crying with a disturbed heart. I prayed so many times for answers and seemed to get no reply. I remember "ugly crying" face down on the floor in my bedroom for so long that I fell asleep. I mean, I was doing all the right things. Praying. Fasting. Staying in the Word. Worshipping. Going to church. Counseling. What more did I have to do? What more could I have done? I was asking my own *"How long, Lord"* question—just like Habakkuk.

I have always been a girl of many questions, especially when I am really desperate for an answer. I ask why. I want to understand. If I continue to not understand, I will keep asking. Habakkuk was the same way. He was a man of many questions. He was frustrated that God was not doing anything about the downward spiral of His own people. I feel the same way when I see someone plummeting (sometimes that someone is myself) and it doesn't seem like God is doing anything about it. I mean, He's God, right? Can He at least send angels or someone, anyone to help?

I'm being brutally honest, here. There were moments when I believed NOTHING was going to change. I lost all hope—where was God and why wasn't He answering me? He felt far away from my heart and needs. That's when I felt most alone, most vulnerable and most weary.

The good news, though, is that God knows. He knows when we are doubting, worrying, anxious, desperate and frustrated. We can't hide our true feelings even though sometimes I believe that is EXACTLY what we try to do. Put on the Christian "talk and walk"— the fake smile.

When we are asked, *"How are you?,"* we lie and say that we're good. We quickly move on to how the person we are talking to is doing. We may be able to fool some people, but we can't ever fool Him. It helps me to understand my relationship with my Heavenly Father when I think about my relationship with my children. I know they aren't perfect, and I know they will question me, but I love them unconditionally as my Heavenly Father loves and understands you and me.

Just like me, Habakkuk was losing faith. He was weary. He had honest doubts and time sensitive concerns. But what did Habakkuk do? He went boldly before the throne of God until he received an answer. Habakkuk isn't the only biblical model telling us to ask God for anything and everything. Jesus Himself commanded us to ask the Father to meet our needs. He says:

"Ask, and it will be given to you; seek, and you will find; knock, and it will be opened to you."
Matthew 7:7

Notice that God doesn't say ask, and it will be given to you today, but He does promise that you will find answers and that He will open doors. Hallelujah! So keep askin' and keep knockin'!

Heart-Stirring Questions

Here are a few questions to help you to unlock the hopes and hurts in your heart. Read Habakkuk 1:1–4 and ask God to direct your thoughts as you seek Him.

1) What is your "How long, Lord" heart cry?

2) Have you lost hope? When? Was there a specific circumstance that made you lose hope? Please explain.

3) Are your debating with God? Why?

4) Are you willing to wait for an answer from God? If not, why?

5) How do you want God to answer your cry? Why?

We've started asking some God-sized questions. This step is a great beginning to find your hope story again.

3
Purpose Through Pain

It was a difficult season that my teenage daughter and I walked through—one of those seasons that you hope never comes, but it does. You need grace, wisdom and strength like never before. You never want your children to suffer, and you especially don't want them to make the same mistakes you did.

I prayed for my daughter from the womb on. I prayed that she would not have to experience the heartache that I had as a teen. I hoped it would be easier. In some ways, it was. In other ways, if she would have had the same experiences that I did, it would have been gentler than what actually happened.

I asked God, *"Why?"* I prayed against this very thing for years. And here we were, right in the middle of it. I'm not gonna lie, I was mad at God. He let me down. I was supposed to reap the blessings of what I had sown in prayer—that's what the Bible told me. As I was pondering the circumstance, I heard God say to me, *"Don't mess with Kayla's story. This is her story and it's yours. I have a plan and a purpose for all of it."*

I was shocked at His answer. I really didn't like it. Although it wasn't what I wanted to hear, I embraced it. If God had a plan and a purpose through the pain, then OK. I still hated walking through such pain with her, but I had to trust God. I had to believe. I had to obey. God had to be extreme with my daughter because she was being extreme with Him.

She needed that kind of love from God—the extreme tough

love to ultimately be set free. I wrote this poem during that season:

It Just Is
What has changed me?
Pain
What heals me?
Tears, prayers, family, friends
Time
But, as with some things,
This will never fully heal until Heaven
And that's just the way it is
Whether wrong or right
It sometimes just is
And nothing can change what has happened
What has been done
What words have been said
Unfortunately
You wish it could be different
That whatever happened can be taken back
But it can't
It just is
And it leaves a hole in your heart
Where happiness once was
Sadness remains
And you try to heal, to forget, to forgive
To live as though it never happened
To hope that happiness can fill
Where sadness dwells
But like I said before
Sometimes
It just is.

Let's continue looking at Habakkuk's story.

Please read Habakkuk 1:5–11.

God knew His reply would horrify Habakkuk. In verse five, it was like God said, *"You're not going to believe this!"* His words were so shocking. He was challenging Habakkuk to open his eyes and see the big picture—to embrace it. God was raising up the pagan Chaldeans (Babylonians) to attack the tribe of Judah. Destruction was inevitable. The Northern Kingdom, Israel, had already been taken into captivity and the Southern Kingdom, Judah, was next. What? I can almost hear Habakkuk say, *"Are you kidding me?"*

The Babylonians were barbaric warriors who were building an evil empire one bloody battle at a time. They lived and breathed to destroy and conquer—to kill. Just to give you an idea how evil they were, their king, King Nebuchadnezzar, killed all of a father's sons right in front of him before then gouging the father's eyes out (You can read about the details if you like in 2 Kings 25:7). Nice guy, huh? Can you imagine having to watch the massacre of your children, losing your own eyes violently, and then still living yourself? Wow.

Nebuchadnezzar was known as a military genius with a highly motivated army because any plunder his men found became their wages. God described their horses as swifter than leopards and fiercer than evening wolves. (Wolves are most ravenous at night after they have been kept hungry all day.)

These men came for violence and gave credit to their god— the god of power and greed. These are not the kind of men you want to bring home to mom and dad for dinner, right? But God needed to use extreme measures to get the people of Judah's attention, to turn their hearts back toward Him. He had already brought plagues, prophets and numerous military defeats, but instead of repentance, their hearts were hardened. God used extreme tough love—but that was exactly what they needed to be set free.

When I think of extreme tough love, it reminds me of the greatest expression of God's tough love ever given to Jesus Christ for all of humanity.

"Surely He has borne our griefs and carried our sorrows; Yet we esteemed Him stricken, smitten by God, and afflicted. But He was wounded for our transgressions, He was bruised for our iniquities; The chastisement for our peace was upon Him, and by His stripes we are healed. All we like sheep have gone astray; we have turned, every one, to his own way; and the LORD has laid on Him the iniquity of us all."
Isaiah 53: 4–7

Jesus didn't just die for us. He had to humble himself as a man *(Can you imagine being God and having to do this?)*, experience humanity (the good and the bad), be betrayed by those closest to His heart and finally be beaten and crucified by the ones He came to save. I recently learned that under Jewish law, scourging was limited to 40 stripes, but during the time of Jesus' trial, Roman law was used, which was much worse. Pilate, the Roman ruler at the time of Christ, ordered more extensive scourging because he intended for Jesus' treatment to be the equivalent of his crucifixion—not the preface for it.

This utter cruelty inflicted on Jesus literally makes me sick to my stomach and cry. Jesus was unjustly condemned for sin. But not His sin—He had none. It was for mine, for yours and for all of the sins of the world. I am 43 and I know how much I've sinned in my lifetime, and I know I have more sin to go through (I'm just being real). Then, I think of the sins of everyone in the world past and present, which I CAN'T comprehend, especially when you consider murder, genocide, idolatry, human trafficking, as well as sexual, mental and physical abuse—OK, that's enough. You get the picture. All of this punishment was placed on Jesus. He paid the price for our salvation with His blood, to set us free. My mind just exploded. Did yours? Yep. I know I take my salvation for granted sometimes, and just writing this reminded my heart of the gravity of such a sacrifice. Thank you, God!

Jesus' crucifixion was extreme tough love. But again, it had to be—and it was all for us. He always wanted to be near us, to be in communion with us. Wow! He loves us that much.

My prayer is that you accept this gift—this gift of eternal life in Christ, if you haven't already. You will never regret it. However, you will regret it if you spend eternal life apart from Him. God made it simple to receive His gift. All you have to do is admit, believe and confess. I have listed Scripture below and a prayer of salvation to guide you. If you accept this gift, you will never run out of faith, hope or love, because it will always be with you in Jesus Christ. The eternal hope of Heaven will be yours to look forward to. And that's a promise.

Admit: *"For all have sinned and fall short of the glory of God"* (Romans 3:23).

Believe: *"For God so loved the world that He gave His only begotten Son, that whoever believes in Him should not perish but have everlasting life. For God did not send His Son into the world to condemn the world, but that the world through Him might be saved"* (John 3:16–17).

Confess: *"The word is near you, in your mouth and in your heart that if you confess with your mouth the Lord Jesus and believe in* *your heart that God has raised Him from the dead, you will be saved. For with the heart one believes unto righteousness, and with the mouth confession is made unto salvation" (Romans 10:8–10).*

Prayer of Salvation
Dear God, please forgive me. I thank You for Your love and sacrifice of Your only Son Jesus to be crucified for my sins. I accept this precious gift of salvation with my whole heart and accept Jesus Christ as my Lord and Savior. Help me to stay close to You all the days of my life. In Jesus' name. Amen.

This prayer is where eternal hope begins. You can never lose it and you can always draw from it. It is a never-ending waterfall of love from our Heavenly Father. I can never get my head or heart around that idea. But I don't have to. He's God and I am just sooo thankful and grateful for this precious gift of salvation that I want to love, honor and glorify Him through my life: my actions, my words, how well I love and serve others, my worship and more, to show Him just how thankful I am.

If you just accepted Jesus as your Lord and Savior, I am jumping up and down right now uncontrollably and screaming, *"Hallelujah, thank you Jesus and AMEN!"* You are an official child of God, a daughter of Christ and an heiress to the Kingdom of Heaven! This is the best day of your life. Write down the date and celebrate!!

This truth now applies to you—and to all those before you who have accepted Christ's free gift of salvation.

"To all who did receive Him, to those who believed in His name,
He gave the right to become children of God."
John 1:12

And NOTHING can take away your salvation:

"For I am persuaded, that neither death, nor life, nor angels, nor principalities, nor powers, nor things present, nor things to come, nor height, nor depth, nor any other creature, shall be able to separate us from the love of God, which is in Christ Jesus our Lord."
Romans 8:38–39

If you just prayed this prayer, please also see the *Next Steps for New Believers* page on page 99.

Heart-Stirring Questions

I encourage you to ponder your journey toward hope as you answer the following questions.

1) What was your "knee jerk" reaction to God's reply to Habakkuk? Why?

2) Did your first reaction change after deliberation? Why?

3) When you don't get the answer you were expecting, what do you do? What should you do? Why?

4) When has God used extreme tough love in your or a loved one's life? How did it make you feel? Why?

5) Are you willing to trust and obey no matter what? Why?

The journey to find purpose through pain can be difficult. I commend you for taking the brave step to keep asking God the hard questions to help you begin to find purpose out of your pain. I know if you are His child, if you believe in Him, that He is cheering you on. Take heart, for *"we know that all things work together for good to those who love God, to those who are the called according to His purpose"* (Romans 8:28).

Notes

4

Wrestling with God

Remember that one of the meanings of Habakkuk was "wrestle?" In Merriam-Webster's Dictionary, the word wrestle means: to struggle to move, deal with, or control something.

When we are dealing with a really difficult situation that we don't quite understand yet, we wrestle and we struggle with it. We are trying to figure it out. We are attempting to have some control over the situation, striving to determine how the course of events should go, and we are expressing our desire for a certain outcome.

Wrestling happens when a mother and father have to walk through the untimely passing of their child. It's when the doctor says, *"You have cancer."* It's when you never thought in a million years "divorce" would be in your vocabulary. It's also when events send you into a tail spin down the darkest black hole of your life. We all wrestle. We wrestle in our minds, with the people dearest to us and with the Lord.

My Journal Entry 6.20.2012—Wrestling with God

Sometimes I wrestle with God, and I don't even realize it. When I want some situation to go my way, I "pray" or should I say "tell" God what should happen versus submitting a request. From time to time, I actually believe it's an innocent request, when the truth is, I'm expecting—no demanding—a certain outcome. Deep down, if I'm honest, this is what the unmasked prayer is, *"Lord, I really need this to go this way. I have done everything in my power that You* have asked. I'm just asking to reap what I have sown. You said that's the way it works. You are my Heavenly Father, who, I know, wants to bless His faithful daughter, so PLEEEASE?"

God gently smiles and listens attentively. He then waits to answer until I can handle the reply He needs to give, when I am ready to accept the different direction, or the no, not now answer that I NEVER expected. Maybe it's an answer that will change the course of my life forever. And sometimes when He tells me, my heart stops and tears fall as I ponder what He has said. In time (sometimes a long time), I understand, I accept, I trust His perfect will and plan. I thank Him that He knows what's best for me, and I love Him and will continue to trust even though we may wrestle again.

"'For I know the plans I have for you,' declares the LORD, 'plans to prosper you and not to harm you, plans to give you hope and a future.'"
Jeremiah 29:11

Please read Habakkuk 1:12–17.

I can totally sympathize with Habakkuk's frustration. First, Habakkuk asks why God wasn't doing anything about the demise of His people. Then, after God reveals the plan, Habakkuk REALLY doesn't understand what in the world God is thinking. I can relate— can you? There have been moments when I thought I was going a little cuckoo, like a screw had been lost in my head and nobody could find it—least of all, me. Nothing in my life was making sense. After my son left for college, I was beginning to feel the empty-nesting blues. I was not the Lona I had known for 40 years. I was the anti-Lona: sad, lonely and feeling like my situation had no end. And the way that God answered my cries for help was definitely not what I was expecting.

Habakkuk was horrified! He wasn't frustrated that God was bringing judgment to Judah, rather he was perplexed about how God was executing it. Why would God use pagans to attack His own people? They needed intervention, not annihilation. Then evil wins. What good would that do? Habakkuk describes the people of Judah as hopeless fish, who can't protect themselves, caught in the mighty Babylonians' net.

Habakkuk continues to wrestle with God about the destruction of Judah. He pleads with God, reminding Him—as if God needs reminding—*"You are a Holy God! How can you use evil? You don't tolerate evil, your eyes can't look upon it! This is crazy!"* If you think about it though, Judah was being more evil than the Babylonians. The people of Judah knew God and His laws and went against Him, hardening their hearts.

The Babylonians, yes, they were barbaric and held accountable for their actions, but they didn't know God or His laws. Who is more wrong? Which is the lesser evil of the two, really? Ouch. Ouch. Ouch! OK, I need to go repent. God tells all of His people about the consequences of turning against Him throughout Scripture. Here is just one verse in the New Testament:

"For it had been better for them not to have known the way of righteousness, than, after they have known it, to turn from the holy commandment delivered unto them."
2 Peter 2:21

The good news is, because of God's promise to His people, Habakkuk knew that Judah could not be completely annihilated, and therefore interceded for his people and claimed the promise in Habakkuk 1:12. The promise that Habakkuk stood on went all the way back to God's covenant with Abraham, Isaac and Jacob.

"I will confirm my covenant as a perpetual covenant between me and you. It will extend to your descendants after you throughout their generations. I will be your God and the God of your descendants after you."
Gen 17:7

Even though Habakkuk interceded for His people, he wasn't perfect—he wrestled. Let's talk about a couple key components of wrestling: doubt and disbelief. Doubt is to be uncertain; disbelief is refusal to accept something as true. Habakkuk debated with God, but He never gave up on Him. He trusted in God's Sovereignty.

We must be honest with God (He knows, anyway) and wrestle, seek and ask to grow in our faith and build those Wonder Woman muscles! I know, it's really painful sometimes, but it will all be worth it.

"Consider it all joy, my brethren, when you encounter various trials, knowing that the testing of your faith produces endurance. And let endurance have its perfect result, so that you may be perfect and complete, lacking in nothing."
James 1:2–4

This verse was the Scripture that my best friend claimed through her journey with Breast Cancer. The initial diagnosis was bad enough, but then we found out the cancer was aggressive and went from Stage 2 to Stage 3. This new information was paralyzing for a moment. We didn't know what to expect. We asked why. We didn't understand all that this meant for the future; we wrestled, but we always trusted in God's Sovereignty above all.

The following verses are great to meditate on as you wrestle with God.

"Oh, the depth of the riches of the wisdom and knowledge of God! How unsearchable his judgments, and his paths beyond tracing out! Who has known the mind of the Lord? Or who has been his counselor? Who has ever given to God, that God should repay them? For from him and through him and for him are all things. To him be the glory forever! Amen."
Romans 11:33–36

And

"'For my thoughts are not your thoughts, neither are your ways my ways,' declares the LORD. 'As the heavens are higher than the earth, so are my ways higher than your ways and my thoughts than your thoughts.'"
Isaiah 55:8–9

Heart-Stirring Questions

Here are some questions to help you find strength through your struggle. Ask God to give you revelation as He gently leads.

1) What are you wrestling with God about?

2) Is it your will or His will you are desiring? Why?

3) Are you doubting or do you have disbelief? Why?

4) Do you need to let go of trying to control the outcome? Why?

5) Do you trust in God's Sovereignty above all? Why?

I hope that you have received some fresh revelation from God as you asked him these questions. I believe that all of us will see that as He continues to give us this revelation, our wrestling instincts will begin to ease up a bit. We are seeing His character and trusting more in His promises as we *"consider it all joy."*

Notes

5
Will You Watch and Wait?

I hate waiting. Who doesn't? Whether it's traffic, a grocery line or waiting for someone to: Take. The. Garbage. Out. It's frustrating! But those are mild examples compared to the waiting that makes your heart ache—like waiting for a prodigal to come home or an injustice or abusive situation to be dealt with—not to mention waiting for love, provision, protection or forgiveness.

I have never been a patient kind of girl. I am also a get'er done kind of girl, so waiting is definitely not one of my strengths. If there is a need, I fill it. If there is a problem, I fix it. If I am in conflict, I want to confront it immediately and get through it. If I'm asking, I want an answer so I can move on in my heart and with my life. God has been the most excellent coach, strengthening my skills in this area. I mean, He's just so good at it! But like any strength training, IT HURTS, and it usually takes more time than you think it should.

I gasp to myself as I think, *"You mean I have to be patient to learn patience? Mama Mia!!"* God usually requires you to do the ordinary before you are prepared to do the extraordinary. I had to learn this lesson during my waiting for patience to bring me to a deeper understanding of love, joy, peace, longsuffering, kindness, goodness, faithfulness, gentleness and self control—the wonderful fruits of the spirit (Galatians 5:22).

It was the summer after my daughter graduated from high school. She was my baby—the last to go. I had sent my son off to college the previous year, and I had turned the big "40." For me, this was too much, too soon. I didn't have time to even breathe from one life-changing epic moment to another. I needed more time to process, to transition, to "live" in my new normal. At this point in my journey, my sadness and loneliness had deepened into hopelessness.

Major changes affect us all differently. Some of you may be thinking, *"Get over it already!"* And others—you totally get it. Regardless of what you think, it's all right, this journey was mine. It was also a time when my own loved ones didn't understand the new me—the one who had changed from a happy, joy-filled, optimistic girl to a depressed one—paralyzed by her circumstances. I was so different they didn't know what to do with me. I could relate, because even I didn't know what to do with me. Figuratively speaking, I was at the shoreline, where the ocean and the dry land met. On one side was only dry sand, like the dryness my heart felt, and on the other, a deep abundance of ever-flowing water, which was where my heart longed to be again.

But, I needed to wait out the tide that came crashing in with an undercurrent so strong that I almost drowned from it. I had to wait for my loved ones to understand, I had to wait for me to understand and I had to wait for help from the only One who could rescue my troubled heart. And let me tell you, I couldn't WAIT (pun intended) for the Lord to give me relief—and more than that, revelation. Habakkuk was waiting for the same reprieve.

The Difference Between Waiting and Watching
Wait—to remain or stay in expectation (of something)[1]

Watch—to look and wait expectantly or in anticipation (of something)[2]

Waiting is resting in expectation, while watching is more active in expectation. Habakkuk stood on the rampart as a watchman, waiting in anticipation for an answer from the Lord. A rampart is a defensive wall. Its purpose in those times was to provide a high, safe place to observe the surrounding area for defense and protection.

Please read Habakkuk 2:1.

Habakkuk's action as a watchman on the rampart reminds me of the "Star Spangled Banner" verse, *"Whose broad stripes and bright stars through the perilous fight, O'er the ramparts we watched were so gallantly streaming."* This phrase so eloquently describes the powerful sighting of our American flag flying high on the ramparts of the fort during the heat of battle.[3]

In Biblical times, watchmen were responsible for warning the city of approaching danger. If they failed to do so, they were blamed for all of the deaths caused by their lack of warning. The blood of the victims was on their hands. We see an example of a watchman's responsibility in the following Scripture:

> *"Son of man, I have appointed you as a watchman for Israel. Whenever you receive a message from me, warn people immediately. If I warn the wicked, saying, 'You are under the penalty of death,' but you fail to deliver the warning, they will die in their sins. And I will hold you responsible for their deaths. If you warn them and they refuse to repent and keep on sinning, they will die in their sins. But you will have saved yourself because you obeyed me."*
> *Ezekiel 3:17, NLT*

Habakkuk used the illustration of the serious responsibility of being a watchman to show how much he understood the gravity of the situation between him and God. He was resolved and intentionally seeking the Lord diligently for an answer for the salvation of his people. He knew that to hear from God, he would have to withdraw from the world and get alone with the Father. Metaphorically, he needed to get above the situation, like a watchman on a rampart, and not succumb to the situation's impending disaster. The wall was his sanctuary, his hiding place.

Where is your hiding place? When one of my friends needs to hear clearly from God on an important matter, she visits a nearby lake. She walks up into the hills and around the entire lake to get alone with the Lord. There, she hears His voice without the distraction of day-to-day activities. When I know that she is heading there, I jokingly remind her to put on animal skins and to eat nuts and berries. But seriously, she knows when she needs to be silent before the Lord, and to be still. She responds to God's amazing words:

"Be still and know that I am God."
Psalm 46:10

And

"My soul, wait silently for God alone,
For my expectation is from Him.
He only is my rock and my salvation;
He is my defense;
I shall not be moved."
Psalm 62:5–6

Here is a poem I wrote recently after pondering being silent before the Lord:

Silence

Silence
Allows the air to breathe
My mind to exhale
My soul to still
To just be near
Nestled in Your Everlasting Arms
Peace
Only Your Presence can fill

Now let's have some fun and get back into Habakkuk 2:1! Wow, that rhymed—sorry, I digress.

> *"I will stand my watch*
> *And set myself on the rampart,*
> *And watch to see what He will say to me,*
> *And what I will answer when I am corrected."*
> *Habakkuk 2:1*

I love that the fourth line of this verse doesn't say "if" Habakkuk is corrected by God; it says "when." Thinking about this verse brings to mind a parenting moment between me and my kiddos. Every year we go to our hometown of Rochester, New York, to visit family and friends for vacation for two weeks.

As my children have gotten older, they have expressed not wanting to go for the full two weeks. They want to get back home to Tennessee to spend time with their friends. As much as I understand their desires, I don't agree. They can see their friends all year, but they can only see Rochester family and friends once, maybe twice, a year.

They know that whenever they complain, I won't be thrilled. Therefore, they may be a bit anxious as they await my reply. They are likely thinking, *"I wonder what mom is going to say?"*

Just like my kiddos, Habakkuk was anticipating that God was probably not completely thrilled with Habakkuk's complaining. But God, as He is with all of us, is gentle when we are struggling through a situation. God knew the desires of Habakkuk's heart were fueled by compassion for his people. And FYI, I was just as gentle with my kiddos as God was with Habakkuk, but my kiddos still had to go to Rochester for two weeks.

Another life situation that this verse reminds me of is when I know an uncomfortable conversation is coming. I go over and over the dialogue in my mind and try to prepare for several possible scenarios. *Do you do that? Come on now, be honest, I know at least some of you do!*

I imagine that Habakkuk probably had inner dialogue as well. He likely was wondering about how the conversation with God might go after not his first, but after his second complaint about how God was handling the affairs of Judah. Can you imagine what he might be preparing to say? I give Habakkuk much credit for his courage and boldness. I mean, it's God. But thankfully, our Heavenly Father wants us to come boldly to His throne.

"Let us therefore come boldly to the throne of grace, that we may obtain mercy and find grace to help in time of need."
Hebrews 4:6

Heart-Stirring Questions

From all God has whispered to your heart through this lesson, please take your time and answer the following questions:

1) What are you waiting for right now?

2) How long are you willing to watch and wait?

3) Can you think of a situation when you watched and waited and experienced God's faithfulness? Please explain your answer.

4) Do you have a hiding place to seek hard after the Father's heart? If so, where? If not, where could it be?

5) Why is silence important? Do you need more silence in your life?

Let us be watchman on our own walls waiting in active expectation to see what the Lord will do. No matter what happens, we will see that along the way, He is always faithful.

Notes

6
How Much Faith Do You Have?

Priorities for today—begin and end with chocolate!

Take a deep breath in through your nose (no really, please do it, nobody's watching). OK. Now exhale slowly through your mouth as you lower your shoulders. My mom taught me that little trick to relax. So let's reeelaaax!

We're at the halfway point of this study and YOU ARE DOING FABULOUSLY WELL, DAHLING, SIMPLY FABULOUS! Reward yourself (I love rewards) and go out to lunch with your BFF, go "fun" shopping AND go out to dinner with a loved one (notice I have two food options?). I'm Italian; I love food and even more than that, I love eating food with my people! OK, enough of that. Let's have a Habakkuk recap:

God Why? Habakkuk 1:1–4

What happened—Habakkuk asked God why He wasn't doing anything about Judah's demise and why He wasn't giving him an answer? Habakkuk was extremely concerned for his people.

A reflection for us—It's OK to ask God why He's being silent, and seemingly inactive in a situation. We need to remember that sometimes our perceptions are incorrect. Silence from God NEVER means He's not at work. He's just working "behind the scenes."

Purpose Through Pain—Habakkuk 1:5–11
What happened—God replied with the tough love of raising the pagan Babylonians to attack Judah. He had warned the people of Judah for years to turn away from their sin with no success. He had to get their attention. When people are extreme with God, He needs to be extreme with them.

A reflection for us—We can recognize where purpose through pain might be active in our own lives. We also learned that Jesus is our greatest resource for hope. If we accept the gift of salvation that God so freely gave by sacrificing His Only Son as payment for our sins, we have the eternal hope of Heaven! Can. I. Get. A. Witness?! Hallelujah! And—AMEN!!

Wrestling with God—Habakkuk 1:12–17
What happened—Habakkuk was flabbergasted with God's reply. He wrestled with God's decision to raise up evil against good because the barbaric Babylonians were coming for war against his dear tribe of Judah. He didn't understand how a Holy God could use evil for anything, least of all to bring harm to His own people. Evil should never be given the right to win, especially by God.

A reflection for us—Are we asking for God's will or our own? Do we try to "control" instead of surrendering, submitting and trusting in God's Sovereignty above all?

Will you Watch and Wait? Habakkuk 2:1
What happened—Habakkuk chose to be a "watchman on the wall," waiting and watching in earnest expectation for answers to his ongoing questions from the Lord. He knew He needed to do serious business with God. Habakkuk needed to retreat to his hiding place to be able to hear his Heavenly Father's voice in the silence, away

from the world and its distractions.

A reflection for us—Are we willing to wait and watch for the Lord's reply? Are we active in our expectation, seeking hard after God's will for our situation? Do we have a hiding place, away from distractions, where we can be silent before the Lord?

This week, we will be studying Habakkuk 2:2–4, which says:

> *"Then the LORD answered me and said:*
> *'Write the vision and make it plain on tablets, that he may run who reads it. For the vision is yet for an appointed time; but at the end it will speak, and it will not lie. Though it tarries, wait for it; Because it will surely come, It will not tarry. Behold the proud, His soul is not upright in him; But the just shall live by his faith."*
> *Habakkuk 2:2-4*

What is a vision? In Merriam-Webster's Dictionary, a vision is something seen in a dream, especially a supernatural appearance that conveys a revelation.

Habakkuk was commanded to write the vision the Lord had given him on tablets. As a prophet, he was responsible for preserving and delivering God's message. I thought it was interesting that the Hebrew term for prophet was nabi, (naw-bee) from the root meaning to bubble forth, as from a fountain.[4]

This term makes me think of our lives as waterfalls. Habakkuk was pouring out what the Lord was pouring into him. In this sense, we all need to consider ourselves prophets, receiving and releasing God's message of salvation through Jesus Christ and the knowledge we have of God's Word.

Let's get back to the tablets. They were to be written plainly, so that everyone could understand them; publicly, so that everyone could have access to them; and permanently, so that generation after generation could benefit from them. Having the message written on a tablet was the safest way to preserve such an important message.

If the story was simply passed down through the years, can you imagine how altered the original message would be? It's important in our own lives to write things down as well, especially during significant events, so that we remember all that the Lord has brought us through. It's usually when I'm wavering in my faith that I need to look back on what I have written to see the faithfulness of God. It helps me stay strong and not give up.

God said that the vision was specifically for an appointed time, in His timing, which usually does not line up with ours. He also said the vision would tarry. There's that waiting again! But God reassures us that when the vision comes, even though it may take longer than we hope, it will not disappoint, but rather will fulfill all of our expectations. Well, if that's the case, SIGN. ME. UP!

This promise from God about His timing and faithfulness reminds me of a time, during my depression after my last child left for college, when I was at the end of my rope. I needed a word from God and I needed it now! I had been waiting, watching, worshipping and praying—doing all the things I knew that I needed to do. I remember seeing that a worship night was coming up at my church. That night couldn't come fast enough. I love worshipping! It's one of the expressions of my faith when I feel the closest to God.

I went expecting to feel better because I always do. Song by song, verse by verse, God met me at the center of my brokenness. The words that the worship leader was speaking over us seemed like they were all for me. I could feel the lifting of my spirit and the burden of my brokenness melting away as a sweet release of joy was returning. I didn't hear an audible voice, but I didn't need to, I felt God's Presence wooing me back to the fullness of Him—I could feel my heart returning home. From His Word, I know:

"The LORD is close to the brokenhearted; he rescues those whose spirits are crushed."
Psalm 34:18, NLT

And

"Those who look to him for help will be radiant with joy; no shadow of shame will darken their faces."
Psalm 34:5

These verses and countless others show us that God is always working behind the scenes. Sometimes He doesn't give us any idea of what He's up to until the right time—in His time, not our own. But His timing is always perfect. It's never too late—or too early. Sometimes, we're not ready to receive the next step. Sometimes, we are ready, but other people are not. Sometimes, it's just not time—yet. But it is always worth the wait. So never give up! Your time is coming! Hope IS in your future! Watch, wait, pray, worship, trust, believe and keep the faith!

"Now faith is the substance of things hoped for, the evidence of things not seen."
Hebrews 11:1

This is a perfect segue into the last and most important verse we will look at today, Habakkuk 2:4, drumroll please . . .

"Behold the proud, His soul is not upright in him; But the just shall live by his faith."
Habakkuk 2:4

In Merriam-Webster's Dictionary, faith is belief and trust in God.

Even though Habakkuk was a minor prophet, the theme of faith is a significant contribution and major influence to all generations. It is referred to in Hebrews 10:38, Romans 1:17 and Galatians 3:11. Faith is a simple message, yet so profound. Some chose not to live by it, like the Babylonians. They were prideful, unrighteous individuals who lived by their own laws and standards. They go about their "business as usual" living in a world that was strictly for their here and now. The Babylonians were subject to no authority other than their own. Their behavior is in sharp contrast to the righteous individuals represented by the people of Judah, who repented after their captivity. Then, they heeded God to have faith, to wait for Him, to be loyal to Him, and to pay careful attention to visions from Him.

Throughout history and today, faith is such a powerful witness for God. When you go through trials, it's like God is shining a spotlight directly on you. Believers and unbelievers alike are watching every step you make to see if what you profess is truly what you believe. In the cynical world we live in with many religions to choose from, people will never stop asking the age-old question, *"Is your God the One True God?"* The most powerful proof that we can give about God is by how we live day to day through struggles and pain—it's all about our testimony.

Will our testimony allow Jesus to shine? Will we draw others to the Lord by the amazing peace, joy and strength we show through our faith? And don't get me wrong—we don't have to be strong, have it all together or slap the phony smile on when we're struggling. We need to be vulnerable and transparent in a way that, while we may be struggling in the physical, we know that God is ever with us and will help us make it through.

We can cry and have days when we're weary, but we are resolute and unshakable in our relationship with our Ultimate

Healer and Friend. If we stay connected to Him through it all, God's Power can be revealed through us as He sees fit. No matter how unlovable we may be, He will always love us. No matter what hurt we may endure, He always comforts us. And, no matter how dark the day, He gives us His light, which provides hope for tomorrow. As the following verses show us, we need to allow Jesus' light to shine through us.

"Let your light so shine before men, that they may see your good works and glorify your Father in heaven."
Matthew 5:16

And

"You are the light of the world. A city that is set on a hill cannot be hidden. Nor do they light a lamp and put it under a basket, but on a lampstand, and it gives light to all who are in the house."
Matthew 5:14–15

Heart-Stirring Questions

This week try to carve out some time and nestle into your "hiding place" to share a quiet moment with your Heavenly Daddy who loves spending time with you. Ponder and answer the questions below:

1) What do you need to write down to remember what the Lord has done?

2) Are you willing to wait for God's message? Why?

3) If you have a difficult message that God has asked you to tell someone, will you have the courage to tell it? Please explain your answer.

4) Are you living by faith through a difficult circumstance in this season? Please explain your answer.

5) What are some new ways of living by faith that will draw others to the Lord?

And here's just an extra little thought . . .

I have my own tablet to write on. The tablet of my heart . . .
I have written I am His and He is Mine. God's Word says:

I am my beloved's, and my beloved is mine.
Solomon 6:3

What will you write on the tablet of your heart?

"My son, keep my words, and treasure my commands within you.
Keep my commands and live, and my law as the apple of your eye.
Bind them on your fingers; write them on the tablet of your heart."
Proverbs 7:1–3

HAVE A FABULOUS DAY!

Notes

7
Evil Never Wins

Ok. Let's get this party started. Babylonians = bad, Judah = good, but seriously backslidden. This chapter is intense, so brace yourself, we're going for a "wicked" ride!

Can I just interject here—lipstick makes everything better! Whether I'm having a bad hair day, if my kids are frustrating me, or if I'm in the deli line at the store waiting forever for a pound of ham sliced really thin, I simply get my lipstick bag and mirror out of my purse and pick my color choice of the day. And, just like Wonder Woman and her big bracelets that gave her extra powers (I own them BTW), the moment my lipstick is fully applied, I exhale, and have the power to TAKE ON THE DAY! So let's put on our lipstick and/or Wonder Women bracelets, and dive in! We are almost to the finish line!

Please read Habakkuk 2:5–20. 4342578015227089

It's a doozy of a passage. You may need lipstick, Wonder Woman bracelets and some chocolate today! Sorry I can't share my chocolate—I ate it all during the last chapter! The verses we are studying this week discuss God's wrath of judgment concerning five areas of sin: selfish ambition, covetousness, violence, drunkenness and idolatry. Yeah, I told you it was a doozy. God is addressing the Babylonians as the perpetrators of these sins and He is using this message as a warning for all generations for all time—DON'T SIN! IT

ONLY BRINGS DEVASTATION TO YOUR LIFE. IT'S NOT WORTH IT! I'm not yelling at you—I'm just giving a Lona paraphrase shout out! God is warning EVERYONE about the severity of consequences for our sin—and to avoid it at all costs. Even though Habakkuk's prophecy is more than 2,600 years old, it is still relevant today! And, I thought Pride and Prejudice stood the test of time!

In Romans 5:12, the apostle Paul also reminds us about our sinful nature:

"Therefore, just as through one man (Adam) sin entered the world, and death through sin, and thus death spread to all men, because all sinned."
Romans 5:12–21

Well, thanks Adam! We are gonna have a talk when I get to Heaven, buddy! So, do you have your chocolate yet? Let's go ahead and break down the verses in Habakkuk 2:5–20.

1) Selfish Ambition/Greed (Habakkuk 2:6–8) From Merriam-Webster's Dictionary:

Selfish—concerned excessively or exclusively with oneself.

Ambition—something that a person hopes to do or achieve.

Ambition is a wonderful attribute to have, but when people's goals become only about themselves, their glory and no one else's, that's when ambition turns to the "dark side" and becomes wrong. The Babylonians were these kind of people. As I've mentioned before, if they could have conquered the entire world, they would have. They gained an overabundance of silver, gold and bronze to build their kingdom. Babylon's walls were 55–70 feet wide, when a standard wall built in that era would only have been 10–20 feet wide. They were greedy! Greed is never satisfied. Its appetite grows with each conquest. It is never enough.

You may be familiar with this next scenario. Do you know people who start off humble in their careers? They begin with nothing, work really hard for years and achieve success. Then something happens along the way. Seeds of selfishness begin to blossom. You may even try to confront them about their sin, but they usually get defensive and easily irritated because deep down they know the truth. They choose to cling to their sin, and down, down, down the sewage manhole they go, sinking deeper and deeper until the lies become their only truth. The opposite of this pattern, the one that God wants us to follow, is expressed by the Apostle Paul in the New Testament.

"Let nothing be done through selfish ambition or conceit, but in lowliness of mind let each esteem others better than himself. 4 Let each of you look out not only for his own interests, but also for the interests of others."
Philippians 2:3–4

Isn't it amazing how all of God's Word, written over the course of 1,500 years, reinforces the same lessons that we need today? I think so. With that in mind, let's turn back to Habakkuk.

God warned Babylon in Habakkuk 2:7–8 that they would not get away with their wicked ways forever. Years after the Babylonians had plundered the land of Judah, everything was stolen from them as well—they did reap what they had sown (Galatians 6:7). Ultimately, evil never wins. It may have its time for a season, but when the season is over—judgment is coming!

2) Covetousness (Habakkuk 2:9–11) From Merriam-Webster's Dictionary—marked by inordinate desire for wealth or possessions or for another's possessions.

The Babylonians filled their chariots with everything but the kitchen sink—actually, no—they took that too. I wouldn't be able to sleep at night, knowing that the material to build my home and the items to furnish it was taken from someone else's home. I'd feel dirty, ugly—like a criminal. The Babylonians had no conscience. I'm sure that they even slept peaceably nestled in somebody else's bed.

It seemed that the Babylonians only wanted what wasn't theirs. I can picture it in my mind: the soldiers infiltrating the cities of Judah like a pack of hungry wolves. I hear the screams of the Jewish mothers holding their babies as their children were slaughtered before their very eyes. I hear the hooves of the mighty Babylonian army of horses riding so hard that it sounds like thunder, and I can feel the ground shake beneath my feet. I hear the men in command shouting out the next move to take the city out! I hear the clanking of the golden goblets that the nobles drank from during a grand feast being thrown into the back of chariots filled with pillage of all kinds. The Babylonians were the worst kind of pirates.

Verse 11 proclaims the depth of depravity that was going on. Even without witnesses to see the evil the Babylonians were doing, the stones cried out because of this evil. In my experience, I know sin ALWAYS reveals itself eventually. You can't hide it for long. It's just like Pinocchio's nose when he is lying—it's going to grow and show itself.

3) **Violence** (Habakkuk 2:12–14) From Merriam-Webster's Dictionary—the use of physical force to harm someone, to damage property.

I really like the Message version for Habakkuk 2:12–14. It describes the content in layman's terms:

"Who do you think you are—
building a town by murder, a city with crime?
Don't you know that GOD-of-the-Angel-Armies
makes sure nothing comes of that but ashes,
Makes sure the harder you work
at that kind of thing, the less you are?
Meanwhile the earth fills up
with awareness of GOD's glory
as the waters cover the sea."
Habakkuk 2:12-14

When I think of the Babylonians, I liken them to the Vikings. The Vikings were also pagan barbarian warriors seeking fame, fortune and more land for their own glory and advancement. They would even target unprotected religious institutions, including monasteries—those Vikings were nice guys—just like the Babylonians. And the violence they executed was merciless. Man, woman or child—no one was safe from the Vikings' brutality. Like the Babylonians, they too were blood thirsty warriors who invaded, killed and conquered.

But like I have mentioned before, ultimately evil never wins. At the end of verse 20, God promises Babylon's eventual destruction. In Daniel 5, more than 40 years later, Belshazzar, King of Babylon at the time, hosted a grand feast where he sees handwriting on the wall with the Aramaic words "mene, mene, tekel, upharsin." Daniel interpreted these words as a judgment from God foretelling the fall of Babylon. Little did Belshazzar know, but the Medo-Persian army was already camped outside the gates.

That very night, Belshazzar was killed and the city fell. JUSTICE WAS SERVED. And accordingly, just as Babylon had stolen for years, now the plunder was stolen from them, just like God had said it would be in verses 7–8. What goes around, comes around. It is true—you do reap what you sow.

If you want to visit Babylon today, you will have to visit a museum to see pieces of the destroyed city or go to Babylon's ruins that lie in the area located in modern-day Iraq, 59 miles southwest of Baghdad. Just think about all of the continued unrest and turmoil in Iraq today. Sin can be a stronghold for many generations!

In our own lives, where do we see the most merciless violence? The kind that makes us look away and cringe. The kind that breaks our heart. For me, it's child abuse in any form. A child is innocent and unprotected. Abuse of any kind will change them forever. We may not experience the level of violence from a Viking or Babylonian, but violence of any kind is devastating and a sin against God.

Let's start to shift away from some of this evil now and look again at some of the goodness that God gives us. This destruction of Babylon is a picture of God's faithfulness to ultimately destroy all evil. His glory and goodness always wins in the end. Whatever awful things happen in and around us caused by our own sin or the sin of others has been overcome by Jesus Christ. His glory spreads far and wide as waters cover the sea (verse 14). Everyone will be filled with the knowledge of our God and Savior Jesus Christ. Amen!

I need some hopeful Scripture right about now, don't you? So let's have it:

"For as in Adam all die, even so in Christ all shall be made alive"
I Corinthians 15:22

And

"The sting of death is sin, and the strength of sin is the law. 57 But thanks be to God, who gives us the victory through our Lord Jesus Christ."
I Corinthians 15:56–57

4) Drunkenness (Habakkuk. 2:15–17) From Merriam-Webster's Dictionary—given to habitual excessive use of alcohol.

Drunkenness is another age-old sin that leads to a full Pandora's box of vices. You could say that drunkenness could lead individuals to every other sin that we are mentioning. The enemy's schemes are stealthy. He will use whatever means possible to take individuals, cities and nations down. Drunkenness works at its own ruination. It feeds on any other vices that tempt you. Many times it is coupled with sexual immorality.

5) Idolatry (Habakkuk 2:18–20) From Noah Webster's 1828 Dictionary–the worship of idols, images, or anything made by hands, or which is not God; An idol is anything that replaces the one, true God; From The Free Dictionary—blind or excessive devotion to something.

Babylon was the center of idolatry. Archaeologists have found about 50 pagan temples in the ruins of the city. One of the idols was a statue they named Marduk, who stood 18-feet tall and was made of gold. Um, that's a lot of gold—gee, I wonder where they got all of it? This example is what Romans 1:25 describes as idolatry, or worshiping the creature rather than the Creator.

Idolatry wears other masks besides statue worship. You can make your family your idol, or your food, your career, your health, the flat screen TV, your phone—and let's not forget Facebook, Twitter and Instagram. You get the picture. If you place anything or anyone equal to or greater than God, it is an idol. Many times intellect can even be an idol. Some people worship their IQ and refuse to submit to God's Word. I mean, really, who do they think gave them that intellect in the first place? I think a big factor with anyone who commits sin is a lack of fear of the Lord. He is a jealous God.

"For you shall worship no other god, for the LORD, whose name is Jealous, is a jealous God."
Exodus 34:14

I don't think that God could make it any clearer. And why would anyone want to worship inanimate beings? What can they do for anyone? The answer is easy—NOTHING. They are POWERLESS. I almost feel like saying, *"Well, DUH!"* But I'd better not. I have sinned plenty. I may not have a golden calf in my living room, but I have sinned in other areas of my life. The attitude you may sense in my words is actually anger against the Enemy for encouraging idolatry in others and introducing sin into the world. After all, he was the one who tempted Adam and Eve in the garden. I'm sick of him. OK—enough about that. Back to other issues at hand.

I believe people invent ways to circumnavigate the Lord. They don't want to be subject to the authority and lordship of the Almighty God. Both are an offense to them. It makes me sad and frustrated. And, the thing is, God loves them so much, that He sent Jesus to be beaten, spit on, scorned, mocked and then crucified for them! And even before Jesus, Mosaic law was in place so that God could have a relationship with His people. Did any idol or other God do anything even remotely resembling this relationship? I think not. My grandma would call idolaters, "stupidones" (Italian for stupid).

Habakkuk 2:18–20 says it best. I can hear God saying this in a robust, deep questioning tone, like He can't believe anyone would be part of idolatry. It's so ludicrous when you think about it.

> *"What profit is the image, that its maker should carve it,*
> *The molded image, a teacher of lies,*
> *That the maker of its mold should trust in it,*
> *To make mute idols?*
> *Woe to him who says to wood, 'Awake!'*
> *To silent stone, 'Arise! It shall teach!'*
> *Behold, it is overlaid with gold and silver,*
> *Yet in it there is no breath at all.*
> *But the LORD is in His holy temple.*
> *Let all the earth keep silence before Him."*
> *Habakkuk 2:18–20.*

In other words, God is saying, *"What do you think you are going to get from a lifeless object that you made with your own hands?"* Why would you trust a breathless stone covered in gold and silver? You can't ask it to do anything for you. It's not alive. It's not Pinocchio—I'm sorry, Geppetto. The Lord is in HIS holy temple and all the world will be silent before Him in honor, surrender, submission and worship because He is the Living God. God makes it crystal clear in this chapter that as soon as He uses Babylon for His purpose, the wrath would commence. I would NOT have wanted to be them.

Thankfully, we know the One True God, and through belief and submission to His Son Jesus, we are covered by God's grace and mercy. We are under the protection of THE ONE AND ONLY TRUE GOD WHO IS LIVING, BREATHING, ALL POWERFUL, ALL KNOWING, PRINCE OF PEACE, THE ALPHA AND OMEGA, KING OF KINGS AND LORD OF LORDS—HALLELUAH AND AMEN! Here are a few other names for OUR GOD and I encourage you to shout them out in praise and thanksgiving:

Names of GOD

Elohim-GOD (Genesis 1:1)—The strong creator

Jehovah-LORD (Genesis 2:4)—The self-existing One

Adonai-LORD/Master (Genesis 15:2)—The Headship Name

Jehovah El Elyon (Genesis 14:22)—The LORD, the Most High GOD

Jehovah El Emeth (Psalms 31:5)—LORD GOD of Truth

Jehovah Elohe Yeshuathi (Psalms 88:1)—LORD GOD of My Salvation

Jehovah Elohe Yisrael (Psalms 41:13)—The LORD GOD of Israel

Elohe Chaseddi (Psalms 59:10)—The GOD of My Mercy

El Emunah (Deuteronomy 7:9)—The Faithful GOD

El Hakabodh (Psalms 29:3)—The GOD of Glory

El Hay (Joshua 3:10, Jeremiah 23:36, Daniel 3:26)—The Living GOD

El Hayyay (Psalms 42:8)—GOD of My Life

El Nose (Psalms 99:8)—GOD that Forgave

Elohenu Olam (Psalms 48:14)—Our Everlasting GOD

Elohim Ozer Li (Psalms 54:4)—GOD My Helper

El Simchath Gili (Psalms 43:4)—GOD My Exceeding Joy

Jehovah Gibbor Milchamah (Psalms 24:8)—The LORD Mighty in Battle

Jehovah Maginnenu (Psalms 89:18)—The LORD Our Defense

Jehovah-Jireth (Genesis 22:14)—The LORD Shall Provide

Jehovah Machsi (Psalms 91:9)—The LORD My Refuge

Jehovah Magen (Deuteronomy 33:29) —The LORD the Shield

Jehovah Mephalti (Psalms 18:2)—The LORD My Deliverer

Jehovah Moshiekh (Isaiah 49:26&60:16) —The LORD Your Savior

Jehovah Uzzi (Psalms 28:7)—The LORD My Strength

Jehovah Rophe (Exodus 15:26—The LORD (our) Healer

Jehovah Sali (Psalms 18:2)—The LORD My Rock

Jehovah Shalom (Judges 6:24) —The LORD (our) Peace

Jehovah Tsidkenu (Jeremiah 23:6) —The LORD Our Righteousness

Jehovah Tsuri (Psalms 19:14)—O LORD My Strength

That's OUR God!!

Habakkuk's patience was rewarded with an answer from God. Habakkuk now understood the bigger picture. God sometimes needs to use unconventional methods to get our attention. God had to use the extreme measure of raising up the pagan Babylonian army to get the people of Judah's attention to turn away from sin and jump back into God's everlasting arms. Wow! What an answer! We must trust God knows what He's doing. He's been around forever, so we need to step back and let God be God. Sometimes we are the ones in His way. We need to get OUT of His way and—trust—believe—watch and wait.

Heart Stirring Questions

1) What sin/sins are you currently dealing with in your own life? (Answer in code or burn this book after the last class, but be honest.)

2) Have the sins of others affected your life? How?

3) Do you believe you reap what you sow? How does that make you feel? Why?

4) Has God used unconventional, surprising methods to deal with your sin or someone close to you? Please explain your answer.

5) Does this chapter help you understand what to do when you don't understand? Please explain your answer.

The next chapter is the one we all have been waiting for, so hold on! In the meantime, think of a random act of kindness you can do for someone who is struggling with sin. You never know what may inspire them to turn away from their sin and begin to hope again.

Notes

8

Worship Warfare

"To know God is at once the easiest and the most difficult thing in the world."
A.W.Tozer

I'm still feeling the effects of last week's lesson, aren't you? Let's shake it off, because I am ready to move on and get my praise on! HELLO Habakkuk 3!

Please read Habakkuk 3:1–16.

I have held this information about Habakkuk until now for dramatic effect. I hope you feel it. In the first verse it says, *"A prayer of Habakkuk the prophet, according to Shigionoth."* Well, I had absolutely no idea what a "Shigionoth" was, so I looked it up. To my surprise, I found that it meant a musical notation—it was on Habakkuk's sheet music! What??

The meaning of this hard-to-pronounce word lets us in on a little secret. It tells us that before Habakkuk was a prophet, he was a Levitical priest who directed music in the temple—Habakkuk was a worship leader!—OK, now I love Habakkuk even more! (I hear celebratory music in my head right now, do you?) He and I could totally be friends! I think I have mentioned previously how much I love to worship. It intimately connects my heart to the heart of my Father unlike any other expression does.

Let's dig a little bit more into "Shigionoth." Strong's Concordance describes Shigionoth or Shiggayonah (shig-gaw-yone') as a wild passionate song with rapid changes of rhythm. Some scholars have described it as a highly emotional poetic song. Sounds like Habakkuk was ready to Get. His. Praise. On! He probably turned up the volume as well. His prayer to God was worship—Habakkuk's prayer psalm.

A psalm is a song, hymn or poem used in worship. Poetry is a unique form of expressing one's thoughts. It is creative—distinctly imaginative—with the realization that words do not simply communicate basic thought. Poetry is the love language of life inspired by every moment in the scope of our experience. It conveys the truest depths of the journey of our hearts.

Seeing the word Shigionoth in Hebrew makes the word come alive:

שִׁגָּיוֹן

Doesn't it look like a group of worshipping hands raised in a celebration of praise? This Hebrew word picture also brings me to another thought: If Habakkuk was a worship leader, there must've been a worship party going on in the temple! (Do you hear celebratory music in your head again? This time add a strobe light—and celebrate with me—80's style!)

It's amazing how far Habakkuk has come. His attitude changed from wondering and wrestling, to watching and waiting, to witnessing and worshipping in celebration! (OK—I won't say the thing about hearing the music this time, but just know I'm thinking about it!)

In verse 2, Habakkuk accepted that the people of Judah

needed the Lord's correction, but at the same time, with his compassionate heart for His people, he asked for God's mercy. Don't we all at times need mercy, either for ourselves or a loved one? I am certainly thankful for it. Now, let's get back to Habakkuk to see how his hope story continues . . .

In Habakkuk 3:3–15, God gave Habakkuk another vision. He was able to ponder the glory of God, which is revealed through creation, Scripture and history. In the vision, God showed Habakkuk examples of several tremendous events that God orchestrated. It was a mini "This is Your Life, God" episode. The following explanation is not exhaustive in describing this section of Scripture by any means. I would barely scratch the surface if I wrote another book about it, but here are a few examples of God's glory that Habakkuk saw to get us started.

In the vision, he saw God's glory manifested in past events, like the children of Israel's march through the wilderness from Mt. Sinai to the Promised Land and the parting of the Red Sea. He also saw events that hadn't yet happened, including the deliverance of the tribe of Judah from Babylonian captivity and the final judgement on Babylon. He compares God's magnificence in this vision to a sunrise. In the middle of verse 3, I love that we see the word *Selah*, another musical notation that means to take a breath, or pause. I think Habakkuk wanted everyone to let the words of the song sink in, to meditate on just how awesome God is.

Selah is a great reminder in our day-to-day hustle and bustle, to remember to pause, to rest in Him to meditate on His Word and to simply stand in awe as we worship. As Warren Wiersbe says in his Be Amazed commentary, *"When you behold the glory of God and believe the Word of God, it gives you faith to accept the will of God."*[5]

Thinking about the glory of God and the faith it brings reminds me of the power of worship when I walked alongside my

BFF's journey through Breast Cancer. We worshiped when we were thankful for good news from the oncologist, and we worshiped when we were believing for the miracle of her healing, which she received by the way—*Selah*! God's glory was revealed from the moment she received the diagnosis to when she kicked cancer's bootie in just one year! We worshiped and praised the God of healing, the God of miracles and the God of extravagant love.

Did I mention that my BFF is also an extremely anointed worship leader at my church? That's right—she's a Wonder Woman worshiping warrior and a champion of Christ! One day, I remember her leading worship right after a chemo treatment, which had wiped her out. It was difficult, but God gave her the extra strength that she needed—just as He had over and over again!

Whatever you are battling, the war can be waged with worship. We war for our families, our friends, healing, provision, strength, protection—for anything. Worship is prayer in song. It is an intimate conversation between you and the Lord. It's a time to say, "*I love You*" and hear Him say, "*I love you*" back. Praise is a sweet fragrance that rises up to our Heavenly Father that He receives with gladness and returns His love with Heavenly kisses. It it an exchange between two eternal hearts beating in synch with one another. It is also an eternal love, like a fairytale with a happily ever after that will never end.

Here is a psalm I wrote several years ago:

Over and Over Again

O how I love you
My rock of salvation
My guiding light
My mighty fortress

My whisper in the mountains
My strength through raging seas
My wind blowing over me
Up to the Greatness

For Your Glory
They will continue to see in me
For Your Glory
The light that shines brightly
Infusing prisms of light
Covering the whole earth
Light we will be, for we love You

Jehovah Jireh, my provider
Jehovah Rophe, my healer
Prince of Peace
Lord of Lords
From everlasting to everlasting
Our Heavenly Father
Who gives continual abundance
To His Children

The children of Light
That destroys darkness
One act of forgiveness
At a time . . .
Stripping away bitterness and contempt
Evil whispers in the night
Will not harm me

For You go before me
You stand behind me

Your protection I rely on
Your love I embrace
Your ear I cry out to
Your kindness and mercy
I live by

I breathe in your love
That washes over me
As the high tide washes over the sand
That once lay dry
Now rainbows of mercy
Pouring out of me
Are Your delight

And as I walk and abide in You
My path is straight and narrow
Your truth will guide me
Until I see you
Face to face
As Moses and Abraham,
Elijah . . .
And I will run, not walk
Into your loving arms
Over and Over again

God reveals His glory through creation, history and His Word. He reveals His glory in His Son Jesus Christ. We need to worship Him in His majesty, in His truth and in His holiness. (Hear calming music— no strobe light this time.)

Heart-Stirring Questions

As you ponder God's Glory, please answer the following questions:

1) Where are you in your hope story?

2) Has anything changed for you personally in your hope story since you began this study? Please explain your answer.

3) Do you have a peaceful perspective? Why, or why not?

4) Do you need God to show you or a loved one mercy in your hope story?

5) Can you think of examples in your own life where God's Glory was shown? Please explain your answer.

Selah

9
No Matter What

"Our joy is in proportion to our trust. Our trust is in proportion to our knowledge of God."
British Commentator G. Campbell Morgan

Only one more lesson to go after today ladies. I can't believe it! Let's dig right in.

Please read Habakkuk 3:17–19.

Habakkuk saw the writing on the wall. He saw the bigger picture because God had revealed it to him. He knew that judgment was coming for the people of Judah. He understood why God had to use the Babylonian army as the tool to wake the people of Judah up from their slumber of sin. It grieved his heart, but He knew that God wouldn't have used such evil unless it was absolutely necessary.

God gave grace, warning and mercy for years. Sometimes the extreme measure of tough love is the only way left to return the hearts of people toward Heaven again. But this tough love meant that his people would go into exile or be killed. The land would be eradicated and the temple would be destroyed. Everything Habakkuk cherished, loved and fought so hard to protect for years was being destroyed right before his eyes. How could he recover from such a tragedy? He would have to witness it. He would have to live through that horror. He was sad and scared of what the future—the unknown—would look like. And then we hear Habakkuk say:

> "Though the fig tree may not blossom,
> Nor fruit be on the vines;
> Though the labor of the olive may fail,
> And the fields yield no food;
> Though the flock may be cut off from the fold,
> And there be no herd in the stalls—
> Yet I will rejoice in the LORD,
> I will joy in the God of my salvation.
> The LORD God is my strength;
> He will make my feet like deer's feet,
> And He will make me walk on my high hills."
> Habakkuk 3:17–19

This passage is one of the most profound confessions of faith in the Bible. Habakkuk found his faith again in his faithful God. He didn't rely on his feelings or allow the circumstances to overtake him, but instead, he depended on the dependable God. It was like he was saying, *"No matter what comes my way Lord, I'm going to trust you."* We know that when *"God is for us, who can be against us?"* (Romans 8:31).

One of the greatest marks of a faith-filled individual is that they are willing to wait. If you are faith filled, you are trust filled. If you are trust filled, you are hope filled. We hope for the prodigal to come home, for the father to stop drinking, for the mom to come out of her depression, for the abuse to stop, to feel loved again, to experience joy and to laugh again. No matter what you are hoping for, God is always near and He waits for you to draw near to Him— so that He can wrap His loving arms around you.

"Draw near to God and He will draw near to you."
James 4:8

In the darkest moment of my brokenness, God met my heart in Habakkuk. I remember in my sadness I was begging God to give me something—anything to relieve my sorrow. He led me straight to Habakkuk 3:17–19, and I started finding my hope story again. These verses gave me the hope that I needed; they were the crack of light to start moving out of the darkness.

He was my healer and the lover of my soul who never left my side, even though it may have felt that way at times. In His silence, I need not worry. I know that He is always working on my behalf, behind the scenes, and I trust that He will let me know what's going on at the perfect time. Though I may be in the middle of my unknown, He knows. I have learned to never rely on my feelings, but to always depend on God's constant faithfulness. He was the One who held me in the darkness. He cradled my heart. He cradled my mind. He cradled my soul. He synchronized my heartbeat back to his own. And the once lost little girl found her home again. Here is a poem I wrote during one of these difficult moments:

A Crack in the Window

I stay quiet, calm
Amidst a torrential storm
That has no end in sight
A relentless force
That torments me
When I allow it
But fallen, I am
Strong sometimes

I am not
So I wait, I pray, I cry, I worship
Until dawn breaks the darkness
And I see a glimpse of light
Through a crack in the window
Of darkened glass
I can barely see
But I feel its warmth
If only briefly
And it beckons me
To never give in
To the darkness
To believe in the hope
That cannot yet be seen
That I look forward to
That I cling to
In the darkest of nights
That I will see

I know I was hanging on to hope—no matter what—at this point in my journey. Where do you find yourself now in your hope story? Are you still crying out, *"Why?"* Are you willing to wait? Can God be trusted or do you still feel like you need to be in control? Are you in God's way, blocking Him from working on your behalf? Are you worshiping? Are you depending on a dependable God?

Please read the following Scriptures and allow the Lord to transform you from the inside out. Let Him meet you at the greatest point of your need—at the center of your brokenness. He's waiting with open arms. Let Him be the Daddy to His Daughter. He loves you. I know that I need Him daily. I stumble and I fall, but I get back up again—and so can you. Allow God to cradle your heart, like He did mine.

"God is our refuge and strength, a very present help in trouble. Therefore, we will not fear, even though the earth be removed, and though the mountains be carried into the midst of the sea; though its waters roar and be troubled, though the mountains shake with its swelling. Selah. There is a river whose streams shall make glad the city of God, The holy place of the tabernacle of the Most High. God is in the midst of her, she shall not be moved; God shall help her, just at the break of dawn."
Psalm 46:1–5

"We are hard pressed on every side, but not crushed; perplexed, but not in despair; persecuted, but not abandoned; struck down, but not destroyed."
2 Corinthians 4:8–9

"Do not fret because of evildoers, Nor be envious of the workers of iniquity. For they shall soon be cut down like the grass, And wither as the green herb. Trust in the LORD, and do good; Dwell in the land, and feed on His faithfulness. Delight yourself also in the LORD, And He shall give you the desires of your heart. Commit your way to the LORD, trust also in Him, and He shall bring it to pass. He shall bring forth your righteousness as the light, And your justice as the noonday. Rest in the LORD, and wait patiently for Him; do not fret because of him who prospers in his way, Because of the man who brings wicked schemes to pass. Cease from anger, and forsake wrath; Do not fret—it only causes harm."
Psalm 37:1–8

"Fear not, for I have redeemed you; I have called you by your name; you are mine. When you pass through the waters, I will be with you; and through the rivers, they shall not overflow you. When you walk through the fire, you shall not be burned, nor shall the flame scorch

you. For I am the lord your God."
Isaiah 43:1–3

"She gave this name to the LORD who spoke to her: 'You are the God who sees me,' for she said, 'I have now seen, the One who sees me.'"
Genesis 16:13–14

God sees you! Don't give up! Your blessing might be right around the corner. Keep the faith. I always say, *"When you can't wait any longer, wait one more day."*

Read about the glory of God in creation and God's blessing for you…

"You visit the earth and water it, You greatly enrich it; the river of God is full of water; you provide their grain, for so You have prepared it. You water its ridges abundantly, You settle its furrows; you make it soft with showers, you bless its growth. You crown the year with Your goodness, and Your paths drip with abundance. They drop on the pastures of the wilderness, and the little hills rejoice on every side. The pastures are clothed with flocks; The valleys also are covered with grain; They shout for joy, they also sing."
Psalm 65:9-13

And

"Be still and know that I am God."
Psalm 46:10

From Habakkuk's heart to yours . . .

"The Lord is your strength: He will make your feet like deer's feet,
And He will make you walk on your high hills."
Habakkuk 3:19 (Lona's paraphrase)

A Heart-Stirring Experience—Creating Your Own Prayer Psalm
I did this exercise and was amazed at the revelation God gave me, so I wanted to share it with you!

To get started, read Habakkuk 3:17-19 below first, in it's entirety, and pray. As you reread and ponder each line of Habakkuk's hope story, ask God to help you replace it with elements from your own hope story. As you write, you will be writing your own prayer psalm!

Your psalm can be shorter or longer than the passage below and it doesn't need to rhyme. I've included my prayer psalm as an example for you, in case it's helpful. As you let God's words about your story flow on to the page, don't worry if you can't think of anything directly related to that line. Just move on to the next line, and let the Lord lead as He reveals Himself to you. Each prayer psalm is unique, and He is faithful.

"Though the fig tree may not blossom,
Nor fruit be on the vines;
Though the labor of the olive may fail,
And the fields yield no food;
Though the flock may be cut off from the fold,
And there be no herd in the stalls—
Yet I will rejoice in the LORD,
I will joy in the God of my salvation.
The LORD God is my strength;
He will make my feet like deer's feet,
And He will make me walk on my high hills."
Habakkuk 3:17-19

Here's my prayer psalm to help inspire you.

Lona's Prayer Psalm

> Though some brokenness still lingers
> And doors are still closed
> Where there are noes instead of yeses
> Where there is no friend only foe
> Where my hope seems like an afterthought
> And only in my dreams
> I know that you are working
> On my behalf and in between
> The cracks and crevices of yesteryear
> The breath I seem to lack
> You continue to be my morning song
> The praise I can't hold back
> On the edge of an eternal rainbow
> Sunflowers are all I see
> And I can hear your gentle whispers
> Of the hope that will set me free.

Your prayer psalm . . .

"Though the fig tree may not blossom,

Nor fruit be on the vines;

Though the labor of the olive may fail,

And the fields yield no food;

Though the flock may be cut off from the fold,

And there be no herd in the stalls—

Yet I will rejoice in the LORD,

I will joy in the God of my salvation

The LORD God is my strength;

He will make my feet like deer's feet,

And He will make me walk on my high hills."

Hallelujah and Amen!

10
Habakkuk's Creed

Drum Roll Please . . .

You did it! 10-weeks! WOOHOO! I hope you had fun, learned, laughed and ugly cried. We all need a good cry—and we do it sooo well, don't we? I'm curious, what did God reveal to you through writing your prayer psalm? I wish I could read yours. God is so good and faithful, isn't He? I love how He loves us!

Habakkuk had an amazing journey—it's one we can all relate to. My prayer is that you saw yourself in the story through God's eyes—maybe at the beginning, somewhere in the middle or at the very end.

Wherever you left your hope, I pray that you picked it back up, dusted it off, and through Habakkuk's journey towards hope, found yours again. And, it's OK if you didn't. You now have the tools to begin to hope no matter what circumstances surround you— whether those circumstances change or not. You have the choice to change the direction of your heart. That alone can transform the atmosphere around you as you:

Wait and watch with trust and joyful expectation because God will *"never leave nor forsake you"* (Deuteronomy 31:6). He can't wait to swoosh you up into His arms, and say, *"What do you need honey? Anything. Just ask."*

*"The degree to which I (Jesus) strengthen you on a given day is
based mainly on two variables: the difficulty of your circumstances,
and your willingness to depend on me for help.
I empower you accordingly."
from Jesus Calling, by Sarah Young[6]*

Witness His glory. See His goodness in all the twists and turns of
your life. God will reveal *"beauty for ashes"* (Isaiah 61:3). Seek Him
and you will find this beauty. *"The darker the night, the brighter the
the stars. The deeper the grief, the closer to God!"* (Fyodor
Dostoyevsky).

There is depth that one can only reach through walking
through heartache. Had you not walked through it, you would
never have gained that revelation, that blessing and that wisdom
that has changed your life forever. Always give God the benefit of
the doubt, and watch your doubt turn into dancing as you rise high
above your circumstance and closer to the Father's heart.

*"Nothing is impossible with God."
Luke 1:37*

Worship His majesty because He is Holy.

*"Exalt the LORD our God, and worship at His holy hill;
For the LORD our God is holy."
Psalm 99:9*

Habakkuk has forever changed me and I hope his story has changed
you too, if even just a little. A little is a lot in the eyes of Heaven.
Just as the faith of a mustard seed can move mountains—your faith
can move mountains too.

Remember this from Chapter 1? Now it's your turn to fill in

the blank. I shout, *"If you don't have _____!, What do you have?"* You shout back, *"I have the HOPE of _____!"* (yes, please act this out with a friend—it's so much more powerful that way. And, it's not like finding hope is a one-time deal. I wish we could go through this study and—POOF! YOU HAVE HOPE FOREVER AND FOR ALL TIME! Um, yeah, if I was a hope fairy with twinkle dust, I would totally sprinkle it. *I can picture my pretty dress right now with sparkles, a glitter wand with a heart at the top—I digress.* There will always be something to hope for until Heaven. But I hope (pun intended) right now, in this season, you are finding your hope story again and that you continue to find it. I always say:

"There is always hope, because there is always God."

Below I have listed relevant definitions with our Habakkuk's Mantra and our Habakkuk's Creed. You can use these anytime you feel yourself slipping into any form of hopelessness.

Mantra—From Wikipedia—a sacred utterance; From Merriam-Webster's Dictionary— a word or phrase that is repeated often or that expresses someone's basic beliefs.

Habakkuk's Mantra
I am a waiting, watching, witnessing, worshipping, Wonder Woman warrior of hope waterfalls!

Creed—From Merriam-Webster's Dictionary—an idea or set of beliefs that guides the actions of a person or group; an authoritative, formulated statement of the chief articles of Christian belief.

Habakkuk's Creed

In a group setting, shout altogether—

We are waiting, watching, witnessing, worshipping Wonder Women warriors of hope waterfalls who are watchwomen on the watchtower of faith, who won't leave our post because it is only our unique voice, within our unique sphere of influence, by an extravagantly unique God that by our testimony and example we will draw others to God and His Salvation through Jesus Christ.

To shout out when you need to personally—

I am a waiting, watching, witnessing, worshipping Wonder Woman warrior of hope waterfalls, who is a watchwoman on the watchtower of faith, who won't leave my post because it is my unique voice, within my unique sphere of influence, by my extravagantly unique God that by my testimony and example, I will draw others to God and His Salvation through Jesus Christ.

WOOHOO! DIDN'T THAT FEEL GOOOOOD?

Shout your Habakkuk Mantra or Creed whenever you need to and CLAIM YOUR HOPE! It's yours for the taking, so take it!

Some extra Scriptures/thoughts for you—

"So I say to you, ask, and it will be given to you; seek, and you will find; knock, and it will be opened to you. For everyone who asks receives, and he who seeks finds, and to him who knocks it will be opened."
Luke 11:9–10

"Yet in all these things we are more than conquerors through Him who loved us. For I am persuaded that neither death nor life, nor angels nor principalities nor powers, nor things present nor things to come, nor height nor depth, nor any other created thing, shall be able to separate us from the love of God which is in Christ Jesus our Lord."
Romans 8:37–39

"Oh, give thanks to the LORD! Call upon His name; make known His deeds among the peoples! Sing to Him, sing psalms to Him; talk of all His wondrous works! Glory in His holy name; Let the hearts of those rejoice who seek the LORD! Seek the LORD and His strength; Seek His face evermore! Remember His marvelous works which He has done!"
Psalm 105:1–5

"For we were saved in this hope, but hope that is seen is not hope; for why does one still hope for what he sees? 25 But if we hope for what we do not see, we eagerly wait for it with perseverance."
Romans 8:24

"'For I know the plans I have for you,' declares the LORD, 'plans to prosper you and not to harm you, plans to give you hope and a future.'"
Jeremiah 29:11, NIV

Selah—Amen.

Notes

Dandelion Feathers

I gaze over the crossing
Of the eastern wood
Lights dancing in the moonlight
Wheat grass swaying with the midnight breeze
Of summer loveliness
Fragrance of honeysuckle and moss
As I remember the day
Like a dream
Full of beauty and wonder
And hope whispers blown
Like dandelion feathers
Floating up to the sky
Releasing the gift of the day
To the sun
Of what was inside of me to share
With anyone and everyone
Or just one
I ponder and breathe
And exhale
In expectation of another dream
Lived on in the day of tomorrow
Like dandelion feathers

Inspired by: Hope

Next Steps for a New Believer

Taken from gotquestions.org

1. Find a good church that teaches the Bible.

Don't think of the church as a building. The church is the people. It is very important that believers in Jesus Christ fellowship with one another. That is one of the primary purposes of the church. Now that you have placed your faith in Jesus Christ, we strongly encourage you to find a Bible-believing church in your area and speak to the pastor. Let him know about your new faith in Jesus Christ.

A second purpose of the church is to teach the Bible. You can learn how to apply God's instructions to your life. Understanding the Bible is key to living a successful and powerful Christian life. 2 Timothy 3:16-17 says, *"All Scripture is God-breathed and is useful for teaching, rebuking, correcting and training in righteousness, so that the man of God may be thoroughly equipped for every good work."*

A third purpose of the church is worship. Worship is thanking God for all He has done! God has saved us. God loves us. God provides for us. God guides and directs us. How could we not thank Him? God is holy, righteous, loving, merciful, and full of grace. Revelation 4:11 declares, *"You are worthy, our Lord and God, to receive glory and honor and power, for you created all things, and by your will they were created and have their being."*

2. Set aside time each day to focus on God.

It is very important for us to spend time each day focusing on God. Some people call this a "quiet time." Others call it "devotions," because it is a time when we devote ourselves to God. Some prefer to set aside time in the mornings, while others prefer the evenings. It does not matter what you call this time or when you do it. What matters is that you regularly spend time with God. What events make up our time with God?

(a) Prayer.

Prayer is simply talking to God. Talk to God about your concerns and problems. Ask God to give you wisdom and guidance. Ask God to provide for your needs. Tell God how much you love Him and how much you appreciate all He does for you. That is what prayer is all about.

(b) Bible Reading.

In addition to being taught the Bible in church, Sunday School, and/or Bible studies – you need to be reading the Bible for yourself. The Bible contains everything you need to know in order to live a successful Christian life. It contains God's guidance for how to make wise decisions, how to know God's will, how to minister to others, and how to grow spiritually. The Bible is God's Word to us. The Bible is essentially God's instruction manual for how to live our lives in a way that is pleasing to Him and satisfying to us.

3. Develop relationships with people who can help you spiritually.

Try to find a friend or two, perhaps from your church, who can help you and encourage you (Hebrews 3:13;10:24). Ask your friends to keep you accountable in regard to your quiet time, your activities, and your walk with God. Ask if you can do the same for them. This does not mean you have to give up all your friends who do not know the Lord Jesus as their Savior. Continue to be their friend and love them. Simply let them know that Jesus has changed your life and you cannot do all the same things you used to do. Ask God to give you opportunities to share Jesus with your friends.

4. Be baptized.

Many people have a misunderstanding of baptism. The word "baptize" means to immerse in water. Baptism is the biblical way of publicly proclaiming your new faith in Christ and your commitment to follow Him. The action of being immersed in the water illustrates being buried with Christ. The action of coming out of the water pictures Christ's resurrection. Being baptized is identifying yourself with Jesus' death, burial, and resurrection (Romans 6:3-4).

Baptism is not what saves you. Baptism does not wash away your sins. Baptism is simply a step of obedience, a public proclamation of your faith in Christ alone for salvation. Baptism is important because it is a step of obedience – publicly declaring faith in Christ and your commitment to Him. If you are ready to be baptized, you should speak with a pastor.

Acknowledgments

Thank you to my God—without You, none of this would matter. Thank you for meeting me at the center of my brokenness and for gently walking beside me as you restored my hope again.

Thank you to my husband, Jim, aka Jimmers, my silent strength, who has daily listened to my stories throughout the writing of this book. Thank you for picking up dinner (and the pretty flowers), feeding Ellie and taking out the trash. I love you!

Thank you to my son and daughter, Brendan and Kayla. You are my sunshine, my inspiration and my joy. Thank you for making me laugh, hugging me when I cry and for driving me absolutely crazy sometimes. Both of you going off to college and leaving your sad wittle mommy was part of the inspiration for this book! I wouldn't know what to do without you. I love you!

Thank you to my mom and dad who have supported me since birth. Thank you for teaching me how to love well and instilling character and compassion. You gave me the wings to fly, from Girl Scouts to tap shoes, to my bass guitar. You always make me feel loved and celebrated. Thank you for being the best parents in the universe and beyond to infinity. I love you!

Thank you to my brother David for leading me to my eternal hope—Jesus Christ. Thank you for teaching me from a very early age to never give up, no matter what. I love you!

Thank you to my mother and father in-law, for your prayers and encouragement. And thank you for giving me your son. He's so cute! I love you!

Thank you to my family who have made me who I am today. I would never have reached this place in my life if it wasn't for you. Your constant love and encouragement has kept me going. I would LOVE to list everyone individually, but it would take another book to accomplish that. I love you!

Thank you to my BFF Debi for your daily encouragement, prayers and crazy editing skills until the wee hours of the night. And for my writing survival kit—thank you for being you. I love you!

Thank you to my prayer team of Wonder Woman warriors— Roxanne Wiemer, Faith Ecklund, Tara Bakken, Kathy Schumaker (mom), Wendy Fraser (mother-in-law), Marlene Owensby (like a second mom), Cherie Adams, Lisa VanCleve and Mary Tao. I felt every prayer you lifted up and I needed every one! I love you!
Thank you to my friends who have made me laugh, cry and want to punch you. You know who you are! I love you!

Thank you to Heartprint Writers Group for your encouragement. Having support from my "people" was comforting. You're always a blessing to me.

Thank you to Loral Robben Pepoon for working endlessly and sacrificially as my managing editor with such a tight deadline. I promise we will have more time the next time. And see, you even have my promise in writing. Em dash has forever changed me— forever.

Thank you to my fearless formatting Duracell battery bunny—Kayla Fioravanti!! As this was my first attempt at writing a book, I had confidence that I wouldn't normally have had without knowing you were there for me every step of the way with your sage advice.

Thank you to Jennifer Smith for the cover design and the illustration by Cherish Driskell. I remember the first time that I saw the cover, I cried.

Thank you to my "second daughter" Karissa Selby for your fabulous photography skills. Really, girl, what can't you do? I love you!

Endnotes

[1] "Google Privacy Policy," last modified August 19, 2015, http://www.google.com/intl/en/privacypolicy.html. thefreedictionary.com, Copyright © 2003–2016 Farlex, Inc.

[2] "Google Privacy Policy," last modified August 19,2015, http://www.google.com/intl/en/privacypolicy.html. thefreedictionary.com, Copyright © 2003–2016 Farlex, Inc.

[3] Historic Present Blog, The, thefreedictionary.com, Copyright © 2003–2016 Farlex, Inc., https://thehistoricpresent.wordpress.com/2011/06/29/what-does-the-united-states-national-anthem-mean/.

[4] WebBible Encyclopedia, "Prophet" Christian Answers Network, Web site URL: http://christiananswers.net/dictionary/prophet.html.

[5] Warren W. Wiersbe, *Be Amazed* (Colorado: David C Cook, 2010), 146.

[6] Sarah Young, *Jesus Calling* (Tennessee: Thomas Nelson, 2004).

www.ingramcontent.com/pod-product-compliance
Lightning Source LLC
LaVergne TN
LVHW051420080426
835508LV00022B/3174